★
THE
BIG
TIME

AARON
RODGERS

A A R O N   F R I S C H

CREATIVE EDUCATION

AARON RODGERS

TABLE OF CONTENTS

MEET AARON

Aaron gets the football and steps back. He throws a long pass to another player in a green-and-gold uniform. Touchdown! Aaron runs down the field to celebrate with his teammates.

Aaron Rodgers is a star quarterback for the Green Bay Packers football team. He is a smart leader and an *accurate* passer. Many people think he is among the best quarterbacks in the National Football League (NFL).

The Packers are one of the most successful NFL teams of all time

AARON'S CHILDHOOD

Aaron was born December 2, 1983, in Chico, California. The Rodgers family lived in Oregon when Aaron went to grade school. Aaron's dad had played college football. He taught Aaron about the game.

Aaron with his parents, Ed and Darla (left), and grandparents

CHICO, CALIFORNIA

GETTING INTO FOOTBALL

Aaron played many sports as a kid, but he liked football best. He liked to boss other kids around on the football field! Aaron was a good student, too. He got As in most of his classes.

. . . .

Aaron has always been a leader on the field

Aaron was a great high-school football player. But most colleges thought he was too small to become a star. Aaron played for a little college at first. Then he played for the University of California, Berkeley.

....

Aaron is 6-foot-2 and weighs 225 pounds

THE BIG TIME

n 2005, the Packers **drafted** Aaron to play in the NFL. But Green Bay already had a star quarterback named Brett Favre (*FARV*). Aaron waited three years to become the **starter**.

....

Aaron at the 2005 NFL Draft (right) and with Brett Favre (left)

In each of his first two seasons as the starter, Aaron passed for more than 4,000 yards! In Super Bowl XLV after the 2010 season, Aaron threw three touch-down passes. The Packers won the game to become world champions!

. . . .

Aaron after Super Bowl XLV with Packers star linebacker Clay Matthews

OFF THE FIELD

When Aaron is not playing football, he likes to play golf and listen to music. He likes music so much that he started his own *record label*. When he is around his teammates, Aaron likes to pull *pranks*.

....

Aaron likes to "photobomb" his teammates' pictures by acting goofy in the background

WHAT IS NEXT?

I n 2011, Aaron won the Most Valuable Player award. He had the number-one passer rating among NFL quarterbacks that year and in 2012. Aaron hopes to win many more honors with the Packers in the seasons ahead!

....

By 2014, Aaron was recovering from injuries and looking forward to the future

WHAT AARON SAYS ABOUT ...

HIS IDOL

"The guy I want to be like is [New England Patriots quarterback] Tom Brady. That's because he has won three Super Bowls ... and has done it the right way."

LEADING HIS TEAMMATES

"I think the guys are starting to rally around my leadership style and the way I do things."

PLAYING IN GREEN BAY

"Green Bay wanted me, and I'm forever grateful for that and hopefully will repay them with another trophy."

GLOSSARY

accurate on target, usually without missing

drafted picked to be on a team; in a sports draft, teams take turns choosing players

pranks jokes or goofy stunts

record label a company that records music and then sells it

starter a player who plays at the beginning of a game (not a backup)

READ MORE

Frisch, Aaron. *Green Bay Packers*. Mankato, Minn.: Creative Education, 2011.

Sandler, Michael. *Aaron Rodgers and the Green Bay Packers: Super Bowl XLV*. New York: Bearport, 2011.

WEB SITES

Green Bay Packers Kids Club
http://www.packers.com/fan-zone/kids-club.html
This is the Web site of Aaron's team, the Green Bay Packers.

Pro Football Reference
http://www.pro-football-reference.com/players/R/RodgAa00.htm
This page lists Aaron's statistics and all the honors he has won.

INDEX

PUBLISHED BY Creative Education
P.O. Box 227, Mankato, Minnesota 56002
Creative Education is an imprint of The Creative Company
www.thecreativecompany.us

DESIGN AND PRODUCTION BY Christine Vanderbeek
ART DIRECTION BY Rita Marshall
PRINTED IN the United States of America

PHOTOGRAPHS BY Alamy (ZUMA Wire Service), AP Images (David Stluka), Jim Biever, Dreamstime (Swa1959), Getty Images (Scott Boehm, Kevin C. Cox, Jonathan Daniel, Al Messerschmidt, Jamie Squire, Robert B. Stanton/WireImage, Chris Trotman), iStockphoto (Anthia Cumming, Pingebat), Shutterstock (Mat Hayward)

LIBRARY OF CONGRESS CATALOGING-IN-PUBLICATION DATA
Frisch, Aaron.
Aaron Rodgers / Aaron Frisch.
p. cm. — (The big time)
Includes bibliographical references and index.
Summary: An elementary introduction to the life, work, and popularity of Aaron Rodgers, a professional football star who quarterbacked the Green Bay Packers to victory in Super Bowl XLV.

ISBN 978-1-60818-334-0
1. Rodgers, Aaron, 1983- —Juvenile literature. 2. Football players—United States—Biography—Juvenile literature. 3. Quarterbacks (Football)—United States—Biography—Juvenile literature. I. Title.
GV939.R6235F75 2013
796.332092—dc23 [B]   2012013473

9 8 7 6 5 4 3 2